FEB 3 2000

PhotoSecrets ®

Balboa Park

The Best Sights and How To Photograph Them

By
Andrew Hudson

with
Richard W. Amero,
architectural historian,
and
Ron Gordon Garrison,
Photo Services Manager,
San Diego Zoo

– Photosecrets Publishing –
San Diego, California

Balboa Park.

Map of Balboa Park

See detail below

Where

Balboa Park is northeast of downtown San Diego, about two miles from the Convention Center. The best approach to the museums is from the west on Laurel Street. You'll cross Cabrillo Bridge and enter through the impressive West Gate.

From I-5 north: Take the airport exit and turn east on Laurel St.

From I-5 south: Take the Bering Road exit and follow Pershing Drive onto Zoo Place.

From Hwy 163 north: Follow the signs to Park Boulevard.

From downtown: Take Sixth Avenue north and turn right on El Prado (Laurel Street).

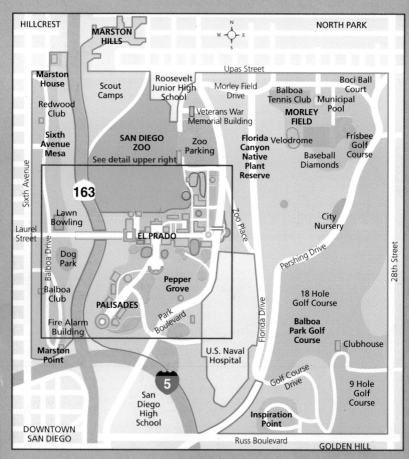

HILLCREST

MARSTON HILLS

NORTH PARK

Marston House

Scout Camps

Roosevelt Junior High School

Upas Street

Morley Field Drive

Balboa Tennis Club

Boci Ball Court

Municipal Pool

Redwood Club

Sixth Avenue Mesa

Veterans War Memorial Building

MORLEY FIELD

SAN DIEGO ZOO
See detail upper right

Zoo Parking

Florida Canyon Native Plant Reserve

Velodrome

Baseball Diamonds

Frisbee Golf Course

Sixth Avenue

163

Lawn Bowling

City Nursery

Laurel Street

Balboa Drive

EL PRADO

Zoo Place

Pershing Drive

28th Street

Dog Park

Balboa Club

Pepper Grove

PALISADES

Park Boulevard

18 Hole Golf Course

Balboa Park Golf Course

Florida Drive

Fire Alarm Building

Marston Point

U.S. Naval Hospital

Clubhouse

9 Hole Golf Course

Golf Course Drive

5

San Diego High School

Inspiration Point

DOWNTOWN SAN DIEGO

Russ Boulevard

GOLDEN HILL

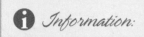

Information:

**Balboa Park Visitor Center
House of Hospitality
1549 El Prado
San Diego CA 92101-1660**

In the House of Hospitality, by Plaza de Panama.
Open: 9–4 daily.
Tel: 619-239-0512.

Balboa Park

Main Buildings/Museums

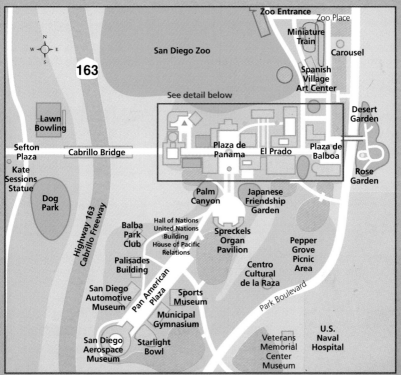

El Prado Buildings/Museums

Balboa Park

With more museums, architecture, flora and fauna than any other city park in the world, Balboa Park is the gem of San Diego.

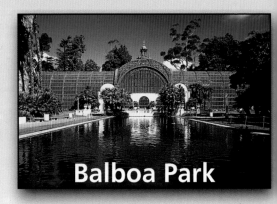

Balboa Park

San Diego Zoo

Known for its pandas and koalas, the city's most famous attraction makes for a great day out and terrific photos.

San Diego Zoo

Acknowledgements

Photos

Most photographs by Andrew Hudson, copyright © 1999 PhotoSecrets Publishing. Many photographs of animals at the San Diego Zoo are by Ron Gordon Garrison or Ken Kelley, copyright © 1996–1999 Zoological Society of San Diego, reproduced with permission.

Written, designed and photographed by Andrew Hudson. Balboa Park history and architecture by Richard W. Amero. 'Photographing the Zoo' by Ron Gordon Garrison.

Thanks to Laurie Krusinski, Ken Kelley, Ted Molter and Georgeanne Irvine at the Zoological Society of San Diego; Mardi Snow, Sue Fouquette and Paul Sirois at Balboa Park; Sally West at the San Diego Historical Society.

Contents

Introduction

Map 4
Welcome. 9
Introduction 10
History 12
by Richard Amero

1. Balboa Park 10

Cabrillo Bridge 16
West Gate 17
Museum of Man 18
   (California Tower)
Simon Edison Centre for the
   Performing Arts 22
Old Globe Theater 22
Alcazar Garden 22
Plaza de Panama 24
House of Charm 26
House of Hospitality. 26
Casa de Balboa 27
Botanical Building 30
Plaza de Balboa 32
Carousel 34
Casa del Prado 34
Spanish Village Art Ctr . . . 34
Miniature Railroad 35
Rose and Cactus Gardens . 35
Spreckels Organ Pavilion. . 37
Pan America Plaza 40
Balboa Park Club 40
Palisades Building 40
House of Pacific Relations. 40
Starlight Bowl 41
Morley Field 41
Golf Course 41
Marston House 42
Tours 43
Museums 43

2. San Diego Zoo. . . 44

Giant Pandas. 44
Map 48
Getting Around 49
History 50
Tiger River 52
Koalas 53
Galápagos Tortoise 55
Children's Zoo 55
Gorilla Tropics 56
Pygmy Chimps 56
Horn and Hoof Mesa 57
Hippo Beach. 58
Polar Bear Plunge 58
Photographing the Zoo. . . 60
by Ron Gordon Garrison

3. Resources. 62

Ten Tips 62
Advanced Tips 64
Camera Stores. 66
Camera Clubs. 67
Index 71

Index to Museums

Aerospace 38
Art 25
Automotive. 41
Champions, Hall of 41
Man 18
Natural History. 33
Photographic Arts 27
Railroad, Model 27
R.H.Fleet Science Center . 32
San Diego History 27
Timken (Art) 27

Publisher's Cataloging in Publication Data:
Hudson, Andrew, 1963-
 PhotoSecrets Balboa Park : the best sights and
 how to photograph them / by Andrew Hudson, with Richard Amero, Ron Garrison.
 -- 1st ed. p. cm. – (PhotoSecrets guidebooks)
 Includes index.
 ISBN 0-9653-87-5-8   LCCN 98-067945
 1. Travel photography--California--San Diego.
2. Balboa Park (San Diego , Calif.)--Guidebooks.
3. Outdoor photography--California--San Diego.
4. San Diego Zoo--Guidebooks. I. Title. II.
Title: Balboa Park III. Title: Photo secrets Balboa Park IV. Series: PhotoSecrets (Series)
 F868.S15H84 1999   917.94'9804'53

First Edition © 1999, PhotoSecrets Publishing.
 Author: Andrew Hudson. Printed in South
Korea. Distributed to the trade by National Book
Network ☎ 800-462-6420.

 The information in this guide is intended to
be accurate however the author and publisher
accept no responsibility for any loss, injury,
inconvenience or other unfortunate conse-
quences arising from the use of this book.

 Conceived, photographed, written, designed,
published and marketed by Andrew Hudson.
PHOTOSECRETS and PICTURES YOU CAN
TAKE are trademarks of Photosecrets Publishing.

 **Your comments and suggestions are appreci-
ated.** If you discover a place or view we should
include in the next edition, please let us know.
You can contact us at:
 Mail: PhotoSecrets, P.O. Box 13554,
          La Jolla CA 92039-3554.
 E-mail: feedback@photosecrets.com

Visit our web site:
photosecrets.com

Left: Discovering San Diego. On the road at
the Cabrillo National Monument.

Author's Welcome

By Andrew Hudson

Photo by Jennie Van Meter

Andrew Hudson is the publisher of PhotoSecrets books. His first book, *PhotoSecrets San Francisco and Northern California*, won the Benjamin Franklin Award for Best First Book. He lives in La Jolla, San Diego.

Thank you for picking up this copy of PhotoSecrets. As a fellow fan of travel and photography, I know this book will help you find the most visually stunning places and come home with equally stunning photographs.

Balboa Park is one of the world's great city parks. Originally a barren area of hilltops and gullies, set aside by a small town of 2,300 people, the Park has blossomed into an exotic playground of lush gardens, shady trees, inspiring architecture, and a variety of museums. In the center lies the city's most famous attraction—the San Diego Zoo.

PhotoSecrets is designed to quickly show you all the best sights. As you travel, this book will give you tips for the best places to stand, ideas for composition and lighting, and historical background for each sight. It'll be like travelling with a location scout and a pro-photographer in your pocket. Now, pack some extra film and start exploring!

Andrew Hudson

2 Balboa Park

"Balboa Park is one of the largest, most unusual and strikingly beautiful parks in the world."
—John Nolen,
City Planner, 1926.

The 1994 Weisman Travel Report rated Balboa Park as the number one city park in the United States. The Report was issued by an agency that rates city parks in the United States based on the number of cultural facilities they contain.

CONTENTS:

Map 4
History. 12
Cabrillo Bridge 16
Museum of Man 18
Plaza de Panama 24
Botanical Building 30
Plaza de Balboa 32
Organ Pavilion 37
Aerospace Museum . . . 38
Pan American Plaza . . . 40
Marston House 42

Home to the world-famous San Diego Zoo, and the site of two international expositions, Balboa Park contains more museums, theaters, animals, architecture, flora, sports facilities, and things to photograph, than any other city park in the world.

Established in 1868 in an era of civic pride and daring beginnings, Balboa Park is a contemporary of New York's Central Park (1857) and San Francisco's Golden Gate Park (1870). Now encompassing about 1,200 acres, Balboa Park is comparable in size to its counterparts (at 843 and 1,107 acres respectively) but contains a greater number of attractions.

The park was little used until the 1915 Panama-California Exposition, which was held on a mesa (flat tableland) in the central portion of the park. Buildings were constructed along a promenade, 'El Prado,' and central plaza, 'Plaza de Panama,' and their fantasy Spanish Colonial architecture has since inspired much of Southern California's Spanish look.

In 1935, a second exposition added more buildings just south of El Prado around a second plaza, 'Pan-American Plaza.' The buildings of both expositions now house thirteen museums, the largest complex west of the Mississippi and second in number only to Washington's Smithsonian Institution.

The animals of the 1915 Exposition became the nucleus of the San Diego Zoo, today the city's most famous attraction. Since 1921, the Zoo has been located on several mesas and canyons just north of El Prado and now occupies about 10% of the park. Although operated by the non-profit Zoological Society of San Diego, the Zoo is owned by the City of San Diego and is part of Balboa Park.

Today, Balboa Park is the city's biggest attraction, drawing many visitors and residents alike. There's a wide variety of activities and enough photographic opportunities to keep a photographer busy for a week.

Right: The distinctive California Tower (Museum of Man) in Balboa Park.

History of Balboa Park

By Richard Amero

Historian Richard W. Amero kindly supplied most of the information in this book about the architecture and history of Balboa Park. Visit his website at:
http://members.home.net/ramero/amero.htm

"These lands are to be held in trust forever … for the purposes of a free and public park and for no other or different purpose."
—City decree, 1871.

"The setting of the park between a vast mountain system on the one hand and the broad ocean on the other is unique. Harbor, bay, islands, sea, promontories, mountains, and miles of open country—each with its own unusual and distinct characteristics, are all incorporated in the park scheme; they form an inseparable and a vital part of it; hundreds of square miles of land and sea are thereby added to the territory of the park."
—Samuel Parsons, Jr., landscape architect, 1902.

I n 1867, businessman Alonzo Horton arrived from San Francisco with a grand vision for San Diego. The great cities of the day were forming city parks—New York in 1857 and San Francisco in 1870—so Horton and merchant Ephraim W. Morse persuaded the Board of Trustees of the Town of San Diego to do the same.

In 1868, an almost perfect rectangle of 1,400 acres was set aside "for a park"—a bold move for a town of only 2,300 people. Kate Sessions started planting in the park in 1892 and encouraged George Marston to hire a renowned landscape architect, Samuel Parsons, Jr., in 1903. Trained in the "picturesque" English romantic style, Parsons developed City Park, as it was then called, with winding pathways and grand vistas.

Developing the Park

In 1909, G. Aubrey Davidson proposed a World Exposition in City Park. In six years time the Panama Canal would open, reducing the sea route to California from the East Coast by 8,000 miles. San Diego would be the first port of call and this was cause for celebration. San Diego's leaders, inspired by the real-estate boom of London's Regents Park and the success of Chicago's 1893 World Colombian Exposition, felt that developing City Park into an area of beauty would bring admiration, commerce and residents—and increase property values and city revenues.

A few months later however, San Francisco proposed a similar exposition. In a highly political battle, San Francisco was chosen as the 'official' fair. Undeterred, San Diego resolved to proceed.

Colonel D. C. "Charlie" Collier was elected Director-General of the exposition. He traveled the world, on his own money, for research and promotion. Collier chose human progress as the theme and 400-acres of on the west side of the park as the site.

Kate Sessions— The Mother of Balboa Park

In 1884, Katherine Olivia Sessions (1857–1940) arrived in San Diego from San Francisco to become a school teacher. She taught at the Russ School, a squatter on City Park land.

When her salary was reduced a year later, Sessions became a horticulturist in Coronado. She designed beautiful gardens for the city's rich and for the Hotel del Coronado, and opened a shop at Fifth and C streets in downtown San Diego.

By 1892, when the land of her Coronado nursery became too valuable, she proposed a deal with the City. Sessions was loaned 36 acres in the NW corner of City Park in which she put a 10-acre nursery. As rent, each year she was to plant 100 trees within the park and to donate another 300 trees and plants to the City for parks and streets.

From 1892 to 1903, when her nursery moved to Mission Hills, Sessions planted about 10,000 trees and shrubs in Balboa Park. Most were grown from seeds which she imported from all over the world— Australia, Asia, South America, Spain, Baja California and New England.

Sessions was the first woman to receive the International Meyer Medal in genetics. She remained a promoter of Balboa Park as, first and foremost, a horticultural park.

Kate Sessions in a 1998 statue by Ruth Hayward, near Sefton Plaza.

Why 'Balboa' Park?

The first problem was the name. In 1910, the San Diego Park Commission renamed the park after the 'discoverer' of the Pacific Ocean, Vasco Nunez de Balboa. Balboa was a Spanish conquistador who crossed the Atlantic Ocean to Panama, climbed the mountains and, on September 25, 1513, became the first European to see a new ocean. He called it *Mar del Sur*, the South Sea, later renamed the Peaceful Sea, the Pacific Ocean.

Architect Bertram Goodhue

To design the fairgrounds, the town's leaders hired landscaper John Charles Olmsted. Based in Brookline, Mass., Olmsted had designed park systems for Boston, Seattle, and Portland, Oregon. Architects Bertram Grosvenor Goodhue from New York and Irving Gill from San Diego were hired to design simple, Mission-style buildings for Olmsted's 'natural' plan.

However, Goodhue encouraged the Exposition management to favor architecture over nature. Within a few months, Olmsted and Gill resigned due to creative differences and Goodhue took charge. He changed the focus to a Spanish-Colonial architectural complex with Persian Islamic fixtures, claiming that this style recalled the Spanish-Mexican beginnings of San Diego.

Goodhue worked from his New York office, visiting San Diego occasionally. His on-site representative, Carleton M. Winslow, helped design most of the buildings while Frank P. Allen, Jr., the Director-of-Works, designed other structures and supervised construction.

Goodhue, Winslow and Allen incorporated details from buildings in Italy, Spain and Mexico in buildings they created in Balboa Park. Believing that Exposition

Spanish Colonial

Spanish Colonial architecture is derived from that of the Moors (Muslims who occupied Spain for 300 years), Italians and Central Americans. It combines rococo and baroque flourishes from the Renaissance with the vivid decoration of Indian craftsmen in New Spain.

The Balboa Park buildings contain elements of missions and churches in Southern California and Mexico, and of palaces and homes in Mexico, Spain and Italy.

Muslim details such as minaret-like towers, reflecting pools, colored tile inlays, and human-size urns highlight the buildings. Arcades, arches, bells, colonnades, domes, fountains, views through gates of shaded patios, and vistas of broad panoramas provide variety. A low-lying cornice line helps preserve a sense of continuity.

"Among the ten greatest examples of architecture in the United States."
— *John Nolen.*

"It is so beautiful that I wish to make a plea: that you keep these buildings here permanently."
—*Former President Theodore Roosevelt, 1915.*

architecture should provide "illusion rather than reality," Goodhue conjured up an idealized 17th century Spanish-Colonial city on a broad mesa overlooking San Diego's downtown and harbor. The cloud-capped towers, gorgeous palaces, and inviting gardens sparkled in the sunlight and, at night, evoked an atmosphere of mystery and romance.

Goodhue hoped the style—eclectic Spanish-Revival style buildings and arcades, vines climbing their walls, and gardens of sub-tropical plants—would supply a festive alternative to the formalized and monumental Neo-Classical style buildings then in vogue for hotels, banks and civic centers in the United States.

The popularity of the buildings in Balboa Park heralded the craze for Spanish architecture and street names that characterizes Southern California today. Hearst Castle in San Simeon, and even an entire city— Santa Barbara, took on the look of Spain. Although Mexican critics called the architecture "Hollywood Spanish," Mexican architects used the same ideas in homes for rich clients and hotels for tourists.

1915–16 Panama-California International Exposition

On New Year's Day, 1915, a fireworks display in Balboa Park concluded with a flaming sign, "The Land Divided—The World United—San Diego the First Port of Call." There were exhibits from various industries, most California counties, seven states and a few foreign countries. The park was a fantasy world that dazzled and entertained, offering a style of magnificence that San Diego could become worthy of.

1935–36 California-Pacific International Exposition

The 1935–36 California-Pacific International Exposition, inspired by Chicago's 1933–34 Century of Progress Exposition, was intended to pull the city out of its Great Depression doldrums. As an added attraction, young women promoted healthful and natural

From 1911-35, Englishman John Morley was responsible for the planting of the park, carefully selecting plants that could adapt to the dry climate.

Today there are 15,000 trees of over 350 different species, the majority of which are not native to San Diego. Native trees include sycamores, sumacs, Torrey pines, and coastal live oaks. Non-native but notable trees include the coast redwood, fan palms, elm, pepper trees, and the predominant eucalyptus trees.

"Botanically speaking, I would call Miss Sessions a perennial, evergreen and ever-blooming."
—*George Marston, 1935.*

The tableau and cartouche on the east side of Casa del Prado, facing Balboa Plaza.

living at the popular Zoro Gardens nudist colony.

This time, San Diego architect Richard Requa was in charge. He preserved the 1915 structures and added additional buildings south of El Prado around Pan American Plaza. Continuing the 'New Spain' theme, he borrowed decorative ideas from Mayan temples in Yucatan and Pueblo Indian buildings in New Mexico. Nonetheless, Requa's buildings are plain and sterile compared to Goodhue's opulent and fanciful creations.

Preservation

Most of the 1915 buildings were of temporary wood and plaster construction. After modernistic replacements were proposed, shocked citizens formed the Balboa Park Protective Association to prevent demolition of the original buildings. The Association gave way in 1967 to the Committee of 100. Led by Bea Evenson and architectural consultant Sam Hamill, the Committee rebuilt Casa del Prado in 1971 and Casa de Balboa in 1982. The 1915 Exposition buildings along El Prado and the 1935 buildings around Pan American Plaza were listed as a National Historic Landmark in 1978.

Cabrillo Bridge

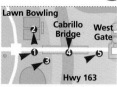

Lawn Bowling

Cabrillo Bridge

West Gate

Hwy 163

On November 4, 1915, stunt pilot Joe Boquel entertained the crowds in his plane. He tried to do a "corkscrew" by Cabrillo Bridge. He crashed and died, five minutes before he was to have been awarded an Exposition gold medal.

Originally there was a reflecting pool beneath the bridge but it dried up and was replaced by Highway 163.

Lawn Bowling 🕐

Clad in white from head to toe, members of the San Diego Lawn Bowling Club engage in their gentle sport. The object is to roll the weighted black balls near the white "jack" ball. There are two regulation 120x120-foot bowling greens, built in 1932.

Where

By the NW corner of Cabrillo Bridge. Games are usually played each afternoon from 1 to 3:30pm, except on Mondays. The lawns support up to sixteen simultaneous games.

Tip

Get low, towards the height of the ball, to get a dynamic perspective.

Sir Francis Drake was the most famous lawn bowler. Upon learning that the Spanish Armada was approaching England, he chose to finish his game of bowls before heading to battle.

Cabrillo Bridge 🕐   1914 Frank P. Allen, Jr.

The grand entrance to Balboa Park is across the elegant Cabrillo Bridge. Designed by Frank P. Allen, Jr., the bridge is 450 ft. long, 40 ft. wide and 120 ft. high.

Balboa Park

The plain, cantilever-style, seven-arched design is similar to the Roman-style aqueduct in Queretaro, Mexico. The cantilever principle was new at the time, but the arched design dates back to Roman viaducts.

Tip
Use leading lines. I love this shot as the gently curving streaks of car lights sweep your eye into the distant skyline.
This is an easy shot to take. Around sunset, stand on Cabrillo Bridge, overlooking Highway 163. Use a 50mm lens and shoot through the guard fence. Take several shots, 10-20 minutes after sunset. Using a medium aperture (f5.6) and a long exposure (a few seconds) will turn the carlights into long streaks.

"The most beautiful highway I've ever seen."
—*John F. Kennedy, 1963, about Hwy 163 around Cabrillo Bridge.*

West Gate
1915 Carleton M. Winslow

The West Gate was the main entrance to the 1915 Panama-Pacific Exposition and above the archway are symbolic sculptures. The male "Mar Atlanticum" and female "Mar Pacificum" pour water from their vases to represent the Panama Canal joining the world's two great oceans.

Above the figures is the crest of the City of San Diego and between them is the date of the exposition—1915. The West Gate was designed by Carleton M. Winslow in a neo-Classical style with sculpture by the Piccirilli Brothers of New York City.

Museum of Man

Also known as the California Building

1915 California Building; 1916 San Diego Museum; 1935 Palace of Science; 1942 San Diego Museum of Man. 1915 by Bertram Goodhue.

"The California Building is second in beauty only to the State Capitol in Sacramento."
—San Diego Union reporter, 1913.

"Behold the spreading dome, catching the light of the rising and setting sun. Look upward to the glorious tower rising so serenely in the sky; observe with quiet thoughtfulness the figures of saints and heroes which adorn the southern front."
—George W. Marston, dedication ceremony, 1915.

On August 14, 1916, Billy Webber, "the human fly,' climbed the tower in 90 minutes. This is not recommended.

The San Diego Museum of Man (also known by its original name, the California Building) is the most architecturally significant structure in San Diego. With it, architect Bertram Goodhue, assisted by Carleton S. Winslow, introduced a romantic new style to the U.S. that has come to dominate much of Southern California—Spanish Colonial-Revival.

Although Spanish in derivation, the building has an unusual Byzantine-inspired, Greek-cross plan derived from Madonna de San Biagio in Montepulciano, Italy. It is decorated with Mexican motifs such as the blue and yellow ceramic tiles on the tower and dome. Everything was constructed locally—the tiles made in National City and the ornaments in Chula Vista.

The building has three main points of interest: the tower, the dome, and the façade.

California Tower

This 200-foot high bell tower is an architectural landmark of San Diego. The tower, decorated with ceramic tiles and glass beads, is gracefully divided into three stages similar to the three stages of the tower of the Cathedral of Morelia, Mexico. The stages change from quadrangle to octagon to circle as they rise. The tower is capped by a weather vane shaped like a Spanish galleon.

Inside is the 100-bell Ona May Carillon that plays Westminster chimes every 15 minutes, and a five minute chime at noon. Installed in 1967 by Dr. Frank Lowe, in memory of his mother, the bells are controlled from two keyboards on the third floor. It takes a skilled carilloneur to play the keyboard, although it's usually played automatically by plastic rolls (like a player-piano).

Dome

The glorious central dome is colorfully adorned with blue, yellow and white inlaid ceramic tiles. The starburst design is patterned after that of the great dome of the Church of Santa Prisca and San Sebastián at Taxco, Mexico. The dome itself is reminiscent of the magnificent Byzantium Haga Sophia of Istanbul. Several smaller domes flow towards the back of the building but they are hidden by an annex of the Old Globe Theater.

A Latin inscription at the base of the dome is a tribute to the fertility of California, reading, in translation: "A land of wheat and barley, and vines and fig trees, and pomegranates; a land of olive oil and honey." Also look out for California's state motto: "Eureka."

Façade

Facing the Plaza de California, the south façade is the main entrance to the Museum of Man.

Tip

Left: It's difficult to photograph the entire California Building ⊕ as there are obstructions all around. Copley Plaza, by the Old Globe Theatre, is best, but watch out for the large eucalyptus tree.

Tip

From Copley Plaza, zoom into the California Dome ⊕ to capture its distinctive starburst tile pattern. You can see the same style repeated downtown, at the Santa Fe railroad station and the Balboa Theater in Horton Plaza.

South Façade

*"The finest Spanish-
Renaissance façade in
existence."*
—*William Templeton
Johnson*

San Diego's
Spanish-Colonial
Founders

1. Father Luis Jayme;
2. George Vancouver;
3. Sebastián Vizcaíno;
4. King Philip III of Spain;
5. Father Junípero Serra;
6. King Charles I of Spain;
7. Juan Rodríguez Cabrillo;
8. Gaspar de Portolá;
9. Father Antonio de la
   Ascención.
**Also featured are the coats of
arms of (a) Spain; (b) Mexico;
(c) San Diego.**

Museum of Man

The Museum of Man
exhibits the anthropology
and archaeology of early
cultures, particularly the
Native Indians of the
American Southwest. It
has survived petitions to
change its name to the
'Museum of Men and
Women' and the 'Museum
of Humanity.'
During W.W.II, the Navy
occupied this building.
They removed several
monolithic statues by saw-
ing them into door--sized
pieces.
The museum contains
one of the county's finest
anthropological collec-
tions, emphasizing Ameri-
can Indian cultures.
Open 10–4:30, $5/3, 619-
239-2001. Free on the third
Tuesday of the month.

The south façade of the Museum of Man has plain
walls punctuated by a richly ornate frontispiece in
the Churrigueresque style. The design was inspired by
the former Jesuit Church of San Francisco Javier in
Tepotzotlan, Mexico, and other churches and palaces.

The doors are made of Philippine mahogany. Surrounding them are statues and busts of people from the
Spanish heritage of San Diego.

1542: Juan Rodríguez Cabrillo (7) was the first
European to 'discover' San Diego bay. He named the
bay San Miguel Harbor. Cabrillo was exploring the
coast of Alta California and was sponsored by Charles I
of Spain (Emperor Charles V of the Holy Roman
Empire) (6).

1602: Don Sebastián Vizcaíno (3) led the second
party of European sailors to the region. Entering short-
ly before the feast day of San Diego de Alcalá, he
renamed the bay 'San Diego.' Father Antonio de la
Ascención (9), a Carmelite priest, was Vizcaíno's car-
tographer. King Philip III of Spain (4) was Vizcaíno's
patron.

1769: Leading an overland military and religious
colonization party, Gaspar de Portolá (8) arrived in San
Diego along with Father Junípero Serra (5). Serra
founded the Roman Catholic Mission of San Diego,
and thereby the town of San Diego, on July 16, 1769,
starting a chain of 21 missions through California. Portolá became the first Spanish governor of California.

1775: Father Luis Jayme (1), who had accompanied
Serra to San Diego, became the first Christian martyr
in California. He lost his life protecting the San Diego
mission from an Indian uprising.

1783: George Vancouver (2) was the first English
navigator to visit San Diego.

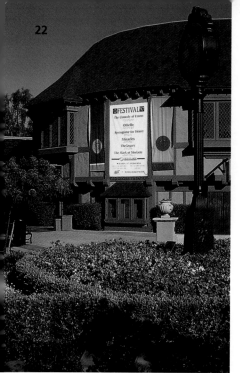

Simon Edison Centre for the Performing Arts ⏀ 1982

Combines the Old Globe Theater, the Cassius Carter Stage and the outdoor Lowell Davies Festival Theater.

The Tony-winning Old Globe Theater is named, and was originally modeled, after Shakespeare's 16th-century Globe Theater in London, England. During the 1935–36 exposition, the theater had an open-air, in-the-round Elizabethan stage where 40-minute versions of "the bard's" greatest hits were performed.

In 1978 the complex was destroyed by arson and the 1982 replacement is a traditional indoor stage.

The adjacent Lowell Davies Festival Theater is outdoor and in-the-round.

Tours are given of the backstage scene shops and costume rooms (some weekends, 11am, $3, 619-231-1941). Plays: 619-239-2255; ticket information: 619-234-5623. Same-day bargain tickets are available at Times ArtsTix (tel: 619-238-3810) by Horton Plaza.

The Old Globe Theater and Copley Plaza.

El Prado

The main east-west thoroughfare is named after the "Paseo del Prado" city walk in Madrid, Spain.

Alcazar Garden ⏀

1935 by Richard Requa.

Right: The classic view of California Tower is from the formal Spanish-style Alcazar Garden. Over 7,000 annuals have been planted for year-round color. Square flower beds with trimmed hedges surround colorful tiled fountains.

Originally called the Montezuma Garden in the 1915 exposition, the name and design were changed for the 1935 exposition to honor the gardens of Alcazar Castle in Seville, Spain.

Tip

Look for details. This small fountain ⏀ is on the east side of the Museum of Man. 'Small' shots like this add variety to your collection of photos.

Plaza de Panama

Plaza de Panama
1915 by Goodhue and Stein.
This plaza, now home to a fountain and a statue of El Cid, was the hub of the 1915–16 Panama-California Exposition.

El Cid
In the 11th century, Rodrigo Diaz de Bivar, a Christian knight under King Sancho, helped force the Muslim Moors out of Spain. He was called "The Valiant Military Leader"—El Cid Campeador—and immortalized in an epic poem.

Fountain
In the center of Plaza de Panama is a fountain which makes a good foreground to the California Tower. Designed by Laird Plumleigh in 1995, the fountain was donated by Elizabeth North in memory of her parents.

El Cid Statue
1927 by Anna Hyatt Huntington.

On the south side of Plaza de Panama is a statue of El Cid, the legendary Spanish medieval hero.

The bronze sculpture was cast in 1927 by Anna Hyatt Huntington. Her husband, Archer Milton Huntington, had inherited vast wealth from coal mining and shipbuilding. The Huntingtons loved Spain and gave this statue and other gifts to support Spanish culture. They gave other statues from the original mold to the cities of Seville, San Francisco, New York, and Buenos Aires.

The statue is best photographed in the morning when El Cid faces the rising sun.

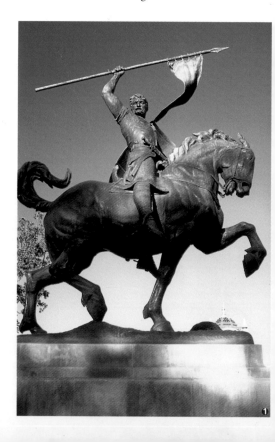

Decorative Styles

Plateresque

The façade of the Museum of Art is in the *plateresque* style. Developed in 16th century Spain, during the Early Renaissance, the style consisted of low-relief ornamentation applied to the surface of buildings. It resembled the fine bossing on plates by silversmiths (*platero* in Spanish).

Baroque

The Casa del Prado is in the Spanish *Baroque* style. Notice the twisted candycane columns on the twin pavilions facing El Prado. Baroque became popular all over Europe in the 17th century, particularly in Roman Catholic countries.

Churrigueresque

The façade of the Museum of Man is in the *Churrigueresque* style, the most flamboyant form of Spanish Baroque. A mass of exuberant and frenetic stucco in deep relief, often contrasted by stark walls, is intended to overwhelm. It is derided as being "decorative toothpaste."

The style was initiated in Spain in the late 17th- and early 18th-century by José Benito Churriguera and his family.

One of the few genuinely historic examples in the U.S. is the 1776–97 Mission San Xavier del Bac in Tucson, Arizona—a favorite photographic subject of Ansel Adams.

San Diego Museum of Art ○

1926 by William Templeton Johnson 1935 Palace of Fine Arts. Replaced the 1915 Sacramento Valley Building demolished in 1923.

Echoing the University of Salamanca (1529) in Spain, the ornate façade is in the Plateresque style. It contains sculptures and busts of five 17th century Spanish Baroque painters—Ribera, Velasquez, Murillo, Zurbaran and El Greco—whose work is displayed in the museum. The museum also displays works by Dali, Matisse, O'Keefe and Toulouse-Lautrec.

The interior has an attractive rotunda with a staircase and carved wood roof.

· Tue–Thurs: 10–4:30; Fri–Sun 8–2. $7/$2. 619-232-7931. Closed Monday. Free on the third Tuesday of month.

House of Charm

House of Hospitality

Tip

The early bird avoids the cars. Most of the Plaza de Panama is a parking lot, which makes for a distracting foreground. For a clean shot, arrive early, while everyone else is still having breakfast.

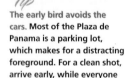

"Woman of Tehuantepec" by Donal Hord. Inside the House of Hospitality is this statue of an Aztec woman pouring water.

House of Charm 🕐
1915 by Carlton Winslow. 1915 Indian Arts Building; 1916 Russia & Brazil Building; 1935 House of Charm. Rebuilt in 1996.

The Mission style east façade, facing the Plaza de Panama, was modeled after the Sanctuary of Guadalupe in Guadalajara, Mexico.

Inside is the Mingei International Museum of Folk Art and the San Diego Art Institute. During the 1935 exposition, the building housed cosmetics, hence the name "House of Charm."

Tues–Sat 11–5, Sun 2–5, $3/1. 619-239-0003.

House of Hospitality
1915 by Goodhue and Winslow. 1915 Foreign Arts Building; 1935 House of Hospitality. Rebuilt in 1997.

The west façade (above) resembles the Hospital of Santa Cruz in Toledo, Spain. It is the only façade in the Park that faces west and radiates a sandy-gold at sunset.

Inside is a courtyard designed after the State Museum in Guadalajara, Mexico. It is is surrounded by columns and arcades in a Tuscan-style.

Naked Women!

The Casa de Balboa has a fascinating feature. Look up at the caryatids (roof supports) and you'll see a selection of buxom women, kneeling and nude.

Timken Museum of Art

1965 by Frank L. Hope. Replaced the 1915 Home Economy Building.

The Timken houses the privately-owned Putnam collection of 14th–19th century European Old Masters. There are works by Rembrandt, Rubens, El Greco, Cezanne and Pisarro, and 18th–19th century American painters such as John Copley and Eastman Johnson.

The shoebox international-style building is conspicuous for being one of two buildings facing the Plaza de Panama that are not in a Spanish style.

Casa de Balboa

1915 by Frank P. Allen, Jr. 1915 Commerce & Industries Building; 1916 Canadian Building; 1935 Palace of Better Housing; 1936 Electric Building. Burned down in 1978 and rebuilt in 1981 as the Casa de Balboa.

The two north pavilions echo the Palace of the Count of Ecala in Queretaro, Mexico. The Casa de Balboa houses three museums:

The Museum of San Diego History

This museum of San Diego's American history (1848 onwards) contains one of the country's largest archives of historic photographs. The museum also displays maps, household goods and furniture. There is a store and a 100-seat audio/visual theater. Wed–Sun 10–4:30. $4/$1.50. 619-232-6203. Free on the second Tuesday of the month.

MoPA
—The Museum of Photographic Arts

Opened in 1983, and expanded in 2000, MoPA is one of the first and finest museums in the U.S. dedicated to photographic art. The museum displays about six shows per year covering the entire history of the medium. Shows have included historic, daguerreotype, fine art, contemporary, documentary, photojournalistic and holographic photography. There's also a great bookstore and a 250-seat theater.

Open daily 10–5 and till 9 on Thurs. $4 Guided tours available Sun 2pm. Free on the second Tuesday of the month. 619-238-7559.

The San Diego Model Railroad Museum

The largest operating model railroad museum in North America. The museum showcases four working scale models of actual railroads in Southern California. Don't miss the model of the San Diego and Arizona Railway over Carrizo Gorge, or the Southern Pacific and Santa Fe track over Tehachapi Pass. There's also a hands-on model railroad for children to operate.

Tue–Fri. 11–4; Sat and Sun. 11–5. $3/free. Free on the first Tuesday of the month. 619-696-0199.

The exotic Botanical Building is claimed to be "the
most photographed and painted subject in San Diego."

Botanical Building

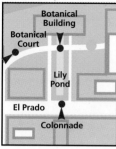

Photographed from Botanical Court.

The Botanical Building is free to enter. Inside are more than 300 species of tropical and subtropical plants including palms, ferns, bamboo and banana trees.

Over twelve miles of redwood laths (thin strips of timber) form a lattice over the steel skeleton, painted to match the redwood. The redwood laths allow filtered sunlight onto the tropical plants and ferns.

The lattice-structured Botanical Building, ① gloriously fronted by two reflecting pools, makes for postcard-perfect photographs. It was the largest wood lath structure in the world when it was built in 1915.

In 1911, the president of the San Diego Floral Society, Alfred D. Robinson, proposed a botanical garden and a giant lath palace. Switching to a Persian style, Carleton M. Winslow collaborated with Frank P. Allen, Jr. and Thomas B. Hunter to design a romantic, vaulted building. A dominant central dome over a narrow rectangle is flanked by two barrel vaults on each side. Two Persian-style domes mark the entrances, connected by a white, stucco arcade.

Tip

Although viewable year-round, this shot (below) can only be successfully taken in the summer. Because the Colonnade faces north it is nearly always in shadow, which produces weak color in your shot. The sun is suitably north only between May and August (best in mid-June), at sunrise and sunset.

Stand on the balustrade (a faux-bridge at the north end of the Lily Pond) and use a 50mm lens. When the sun is near to setting, the buildings become a creamy-gold and the long shadows accentuate the rich ornamentation.

The best time is when there's no wind and the three aerating fountains are off. Then the water is calm and produces a peaceful reflection.

The Botanical Building has an open, steel frame, a style popular in late 19th century Exposition work. The most famous example is the Eiffel Tower in Paris. The Botanical Building was never the chassis of a Santa Fe railroad station, as has been alleged.

Fri–Wed 10–4, closed Thur. Free. 619-692-4916.

Lily Pond

This view (below) is one of the prettiest shots of San Diego. The Lily Pond reflects the elegant castle-like towers of the Casa de Balboa (left) and the House of Hospitality (right), joined by the Colonnade.

The Lily Pond is 193 x 43 feet and is home to lilies, lotus, turtles and Japanese Koi fish. The lilies bloom in late spring.

Colonnade ⏱
1915 by Frank P. Allen, Jr.

Facing the Botanical Building, the Romanesque Colonnade connects the House of Hospitality to the Casa de Balboa.

The Lily Pond, reflecting the Casa de Balboa and House of Hospitality.

Plaza de Balboa

Reuben H. Fleet Space Theater and Science Center

After the Zoo, the Space Theater is the most attended institution in the park. Built in 1967 and expanded in 1997, the museum has hands-on science exhibits and an interesting store. IMAX® films are shown on a 76-foot, wrap-around dome. 9:30a.m. to 9:30p.m. (10:30p.m. in summer). $7.50/$4. Free on the first Tuesday of the month. 619-238-1233.

The fountain makes a good backdrop.

Bea Evenson Fountain ⏲ 1972

Surrounded by a 200-foot wide wading pool popular with children, this fountain spurts water up to 60 feet into the air. On windy days, the water pressure is automatically reduced (via a wind regulator on the roof of the Natural History Museum) so that the water doesn't wet people on the perimeter walkway.

The fountain was named in 1981 after Bea Evenson, who spearheaded the "Committee of 100" to protect and rebuild the Spanish style buildings in Balboa Park.

Balboa Park

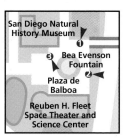

San Diego Natural History Museum 🕐

1933 by William Templeton Johnson. Expanded in 2000. Replaced the 1915 Southern California Counties Building / Women's Club Building.

The Natural History Museum exhibits fossils, dinosaur skeletons and rocks. In the entrance is a 43-foot Foucault's Pendulum, which swings in a stationary plane while the earth moves around it.

The monumental Italianate style building has a mixture of mythological and naturalistic motifs around the entrance and on the parapet.

$6/2, 9:30–4:30, free first Tues. 619-232-3821.

Tip

Use backlighting for fountains. Although most of the time you want light on the front of your subject, there are a few times when light from the back (i.e. you are shooting into the sun) is better. Grass and water often look more interesting when backlit.

With backlighting, the sun highlights the spray and reflects off the water's surface. Like a true Spanish fountain, the Bea Evenson Fountain 🕐 is designed for people to interact with it. Children love to run and splash in the wading pool during the hot summer months.

The Firemen's Ball

In 1925, the predecessor to the Natural History Museum hosted the annual Firemen's Ball. A few hours before the event, the furnace overheated and the building burnt to the ground. Instead of dancing and drinking, the firemen had to spend the night fighting the blaze.

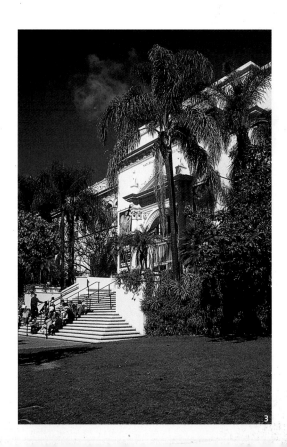

Moreton Bay Fig Tree ⏱

This huge tree has a spread of 120 feet. Imported from Australia, the tree was planted in 1914 as part of a formal garden.

Carousel ⏱   1910

Built by Herschell-Spillman, this is one of only seven such carousels operating today. It was installed in the Park in 1922. Children can ride a hand-carved sea serpent, giraffe, frog, zebra, ostrich, lion, or horse (with real hair). Grab the elusive brass ring and win a free ride! Summer weekdays 1–5, weekends 11–5:30, winter weekends noon–6. $1.25. 619-460-9000.

Casa del Prado ⏱   1915

1915 by Carlton Winslow. 1915 Varied Industries & Food Products Building; 1916 Foreign & Domestic Industries Building; 1935 Palace of Food & Beverages. Rebuilt in 1971 as the Casa del Prado.

The south wing of the Casa del Prado has two Baroque façades on the north side of El Prado and one facing Plaza de Balboa. The latter is the most photogenic. Via a colonnade and courtyard, the south wing is connected to the 650-seat Casa del Prado Theater (above), also known as the Junior Theater.

Spanish Village Art Center ⏱   1935

The Center is an artist's colony where local potters, painters, jewelers and glass-blowers show their wares and teach their skills. Surrounding a painted patio are 36 small studios with red-tiled roofs. Open 11–4, free. 619-233-9050. Adjacent is the Photographic Arts building which is used by several camera clubs.

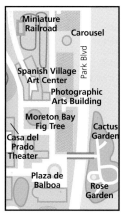

Miniature Railroad
A 1/5 scale model of a General Motors "F-3" diesel locomotive can carry 48 passengers around a 2,200-foot track. Operated since 1948. Sat, Sun hols, 11–5, $1.25. 239-4748, operate on weekends, 11–5, $1.

Tip
Pick a detail. You can't photograph all 1,850 roses so select just one. I used a long lens and a simple background for this delicate portrait (above). A wide-angle lens helped emphasize the shape of this plump cactus (right).

A**cross Park Boulevard** from Balboa Plaza, via a pedestrian bridge, are two attractive and serene gardens.

Rose Garden ⏱ 1975
The Rose Garden displays over 1,850 rose bushes, representing 156 different varieties. There are several walkways, a fountain and a shady arbor. The Garden is a popular wedding site. The roses are best photographed in the spring.

Cactus Garden ⏱ 1977
The Cactus Garden contains over 150 species (1,300 plants) of cacti and other desert plants from North and South America. Peak blooms are between January and March.

Spreckels Organ Pavilion

Plaza de Panama

Palm Canyon

N W E S

Arena

Pavilion

Spreckels Organ

The Spreckels Organ is the largest outdoor musical instrument in the world. This unique symphonic concert organ contains 73 ranks of 4,445 pipes, from 1-1/2 inches to 32-feet long.

Since pipe organs go out of tune when the air temperature changes, San Diego, with its even climate, is one of the few cities in the world where an outdoor organ is practical.

The organ was built by the Austin Brothers of Hartford, Connecticut and donated to the people of San Diego by Adolph and John D. Spreckels in 1915. Except during WWII, the organ has been played once a week since then.

The organ is built into a Neo-Classical pavilion with a curving Corinthian peristyle, designed in 1915 by Harrison Albright. The

Flowers decorate the driveway to the Organ Pavilion.

2,400-seat arena is criticized for facing north, where the sun shines directly in the faces of the audience, but this keeps the organ out of direct sunlight.

There is a free hour-long recital every Sunday at 2pm. You can take dusks shots during the International Summer Organ Festival (Jul–Aug, Mondays at 8pm).

Aerospace Museum

San Diego Aerospace Museum 🕐

1935 by Walter Dorwin Teague. 1935 Ford Building; 1936 Palace of Transportation.

"A significant example of the futuristic 'Modern' styling of the 1930s."
—Aaron Gallup.

"A giant washing machine."
—James Britton II.

The Ford Motor Company sponsored this "ultra-modern" circular building for the 1935 fair. The 90-foot tower was designed to look like a gearwheel laid on its side, and the fountain inside the patio was designed to look like the Ford V-8 emblem.

The design was inspired by Albert Kahn's Ford Building at the 1933–34 Chicago Century of Progress.

After the fair, proposed uses included a roller skating rink (1937), library (1937), armory (1938), rifle range (1948), aquatic coliseum (1950), home for the Museum of Man (1957), fallout shelter (1960), and an aerospace museum (1972).

The doughnut-shaped building is packed with original and replica aircraft, from the early days to space flight. Included are replicas of the Red Barron's WWI Fokker Dr. I Triplane and, as a centerpiece, Lindbergh's *Spirit of St. Louis.*

Open: 10–4:30/5:30. $6/$2. Free on the fourth Tuesday of the month. 619-234-8291.

Tip
Use humor. This shot of the Aerospace Museum comes alive due to the plane flying overhead. It's easy to capture as, aptly enough, the museum is under the flight path to San Diego airport.

The A-12 Blackbird reconnaissance plane (precursor to the SR-71 Blackbird) makes a dynamic foreground. Use a wide-angle lens (35mm) to make the Blackbird jump out of the shot.

Charles Lindbergh and the *Spirit of St. Louis*

The *Spirit of St. Louis* was built in San Diego, about a mile west of the museum, near today's Lindbergh

Field airport. It was built by T. Claude Ryan and his company, Ryan Aeronautics.

Ryan was an airmail pilot from Kansas who operated a small fleet of biplanes flying passengers to Los Angeles. He had patented and built the M-1 open-cockpit monoplane which gained fame as a fast airmail plane.

"I shall take the wings of the morning, and fly to the uttermost ends of the sea."
—*Charles Lindbergh.*

"What a beautiful machine it is, trim and slender gleaming in its silver coat."
—*Charles Lindbergh*

In 1927, Charles 'Slim' Lindbergh was the chief airmail pilot between St. Louis and Chicago. He wanted to compete for the Ortieg Prize, a $25,000 award for the first non-stop flight from New York to Paris. The were many syndicates competing and time was of the essence.

Impressed with the M-1, Lindbergh raised the money to have a modified version custom built. After an exchange of telegrams, Ryan built the plane in 60 days for $6,000. It was fitted with a Wright Whirlwind J-5C engine.

Lindbergh picked the plane up in San Diego, flew it to New York and then to France. He touched down in Paris on May 21, 1927, after a 33 1/2 hour flight.

Returning to San Diego, Lindbergh was honored with a great dinner at the Hotel del Coronado. Several towns were named after Lindbergh and he became the first *Man of the Year* for Time magazine.

Ryan continued building aircraft. He designed the Ryan ST, a popular training monoplane, and the Ryan X-13 vertical take-off plane.

Pan America Plaza

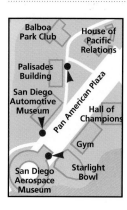

Tip

Find a complementing foreground. **For this shot of the southwestern-style Balboa Park Club, I used the cacti by the Puppet Theater to complement and offset the architecture. Now you could be in Santa Fe rather than San Diego!**

To emphasize the cactus, I crouched low and close to the leaves, and used a 28mm lens set to f22 (to keep everything in focus). The tree in the top left helps to frame the shot.

House of Pacific Relations

A cluster of fifteen cottages from the 1935 Exposition represent thirty-one nationality groups. Cottages are open Sunday and first Tuesday of each month, about 12–2. On summer Sundays there are 30-minute displays of native music and dancing on the lawn. Sunday 2–3p.m. summer (Mar–Oct). **619-234-0739.**

Balboa Park Club ☉

1915 by the Rapp Brothers. 1915 New Mexico State Building; 1935 Palace of Education.

A striking Pueblo-Revival style building complete with vigas (wooden tree stumps) that protrude from the walls. It was based on the Church of San Esteban del Rey at Acoma.

Palisades Building ☉

Adjacent to the Balboa Park Club is the similar Palisades Building which contains a recital hall and the Marie Hitchcock Puppet Theater for children. It was originally known as "The Woman's Palace."

Tel: 619-685-5045.

San Diego Auto-motive Museum

1935 Conference Building.
The museum exhibits over 70 historic automobiles and motorcycles. Look out for the 1948 Tucker "Torpe-do," 1932 Rolls Royce, and Steve McQueen's 1934 Packard that he drove with his dog in the rumble seat.
The building is inspired by Mayan temples.
9/10–4:30/5:30 $6/$2. Free fourth Tues. of the month.
619-231-2886.

A 1929 Isotta Franchini, which cost the price of ten Buicks.

Starlight Bowl

1935 Ford Bowl
In the summer, the Starlight Musical Theater and San Diego Civic Light Opera pre-sent performances in this 4,324-seat, open-air bowl.
619-544-7800.

Balboa Park Golf Course ⏱

Right: The "19th Hole" club-house has a sweeping view of the course's final hole and the San Diego skyline.

San Diego Hall of Champions

1935 Federal Building

A sports museum highlighting the achievements of San Diego County athletes. The building was modeled after the Palace of the Governor in Uxmal, Yucatan, Mexico.

Morley Field ⏱

Occupying the eastern third of Balboa Park is a municipal sports complex. There's a swimming pool, velodrome, archery range, several baseball diamonds, 25 tennis courts, two public golf courses, and a Frisbee golf course. The Field named after John Morley, from Derbyshire, England, who was the park's superin-tendent from 1911 to 1939, during both expositions.

Marston House

Tip

Grass is good. Although Gordon Gecko in the movie "Wall Street" said "greed is good," I think his photographer alter-ego would favor grass. It's simple, pastoral, and makes the perfect foreground for this craftsman-style house. This shot is taken from the rear of the house, just as the lawn reaches the trees.

Nearby

Mission Hills was promoted as an upscale neighborhood and contains several notable houses. Richard Requa's house (1911) is at 4346 Valle Vista; William Templeton Johnson: 4520 Trias Street; Kate Sessions: Montecito and Lark streets.

"Within its spreading mesas and rugged picturesque canyons, there is nothing else like it among the parks of the world."
—Samuel Parsons, Jr.

Marston House

The George White and Anna Gunn Marston House lies on the north-west corner of Balboa Park.

The 21-room house and 4 1/2 acre estate was the home of George W. Marston (1850-1946), a civic leader and philanthropist. Marston worked at Alonzo Horton's hotel as a clerk before founding a department store. At its height, The Marston Company occupied a five-story building on Fifth Avenue and was the premier place to shop in San Diego. Marston helped develop Balboa Park, founded the San Diego Historical Society, and preserved Presidio Hill.

The house is a fine example of the American Craftsman or Arts & Crafts style and was designed in 1904 by San Diego architects William S. Hebbard and Irving Gill. Inside, the museum contains furnishings and decorations from the Arts and Crafts movement.

3525 7th Avenue. Open Sat and Sun, noon–4:30. One-hour tours. $3 ($4 with gardens)/free. Joint ticket with Villa Montezuma. Tel: 619-298-3142

Tours

Architectural Heritage Tours. First Wednesday of the month. 9:30am from the Visitor Information Center. 619-223-6566.

Balboa Birders Guided Walks. First Thursday of the month. Locations and times vary. 619-232-6566.

Canyoneers Guided Nature Walks. Flora, fauna and geology walks on weekends. 619-232-3821.

House of Pacific Relations Lawn Programs. Each Sunday (March–October) is a display of folk dancing, music and traditional costumes, featuring of one of 31 nations. 619-292-8592.

Offshoot Tours. Saturdays (except December) at 10am, from the Botanical Building. First Saturday of each month: Balboa Park history; second Saturday: palm trees; third Saturday: other trees; fourth Saturday: desert vegetation. 619-235-1122.

Ranger-led Tours. Wednesdays at noon from the Visitor Information Center. History and botany. 619-235-1122.

The *15* Museums of Balboa Park

Most of Balboa Park's museums offer free admission at least one day per month. (Donations may be requested. Admission may be charged for special exhibits.)

Always free:
- Timken Museum of Art
- Centro Cultural de la Raza
- Veterans Memorial Center Museum

First Tuesday:
- San Diego Model Railroad Museum
- San Diego Natural History Museum
- Reuben H. Fleet Science Center

Second Tuesday:
- Museum of Photographic Arts
- San Diego Hall of Champions Sports Museum
- Museum of San Diego History

Third Tuesday:
- San Diego Museum of Art
- San Diego Museum of Man
- Mingei International Museum

Fourth Tuesday:
- San Diego Aerospace Museum
- San Diego Automotive Museum

Not free:
- Marston House Museum

1 San Diego Zoo®

Above and right: Female Bai Yun is the more playful of the Zoo's two giant pandas.

"A zoo is just about the most fascinating place in the world."
—Dr. Harry M. Wegeforth, founder of the San Diego Zoo.

Where

In Balboa Park, north of downtown. Access via Park Boulevard or Pershing Drive.

When ⏱

Opens at 9am (may be 7:30am in summer); closing times vary between 4pm (winter) and 9pm (summer).

Cost

$16/$7. Deluxe package with bus tour, aerial tram and children's zoo: $19/$11. Subject to change. Call 619-234-3153 for current information.

CONTENTS:

Map 48
Getting Around 49
History 50
Tiger River 52
Children's Zoo 53
Gorilla Tropics 56
Horn & Hoof Mesa 57
Hippo Beach 58
Polar Bear Plunge 58
Photography 60

The 'World-Famous' San Diego Zoo® is the city's best-known attraction and one of the largest and most famous zoos in the world. San Diego's ideal climate allows the animals to be displayed outdoors all year round. Instead of barred cages, many animals are displayed in open, moated enclosures, similar to their natural environment.

Over 4,000 animals of 800 species are exhibited, including the only pair of pandas in the U.S., the largest koala colony outside of Australia, and Galapagos tortoises. Other highlights include two of the world's largest walk-through aviaries, Polar Bear Plunge, Hippo Beach, Gorilla Tropics, Tiger River, Pygmy Chimps at Bonobo Road and Sun Bear Forest.

The Zoo is set in 100 subtropical acres, beautifully landscaped with more than 6,500 varieties of plants including towering eucalyptus, graceful palms, bird-of-paradise and hibiscus. The plants create the natural environments for many animals and, for some, provide the leaves and fruit of their native habitats.

The Zoo has a "second campus," the 2,200-acre *San Diego Wild Animal Park,* 30 miles north.

Giant Pandas ⏱

San Diego Zoo is home to the only giant panda pair in the U.S. Bai Yun (female) and Shi Shi (male)

> **Tip**
> Find a handrail for support. For sharp images you need to keep your camera steady. Since the animals are often moving, a tripod is generally more trouble than it's worth. Instead use a wall or handrail.

are on a 12-year loan from China and are treated as VIPs (Very Important Pandas). There are less than 1,000 pandas in the world and only 16 outside China.

> **Tip**

Be patient. The pandas are shy and operate on their own schedule. Exhibit times are posted at the zoo's entrance. The pandas are most active in the morning, particularly at feeding time. The best shots capture a glint of light in the panda's dark eyes.

Zoo

Faces of the San Diego Zoo

This page: Indo Chinese tiger. Opposite from top left: pygmy chimpanzee baby; Sumatran orangutan; male lowland gorilla; Alaskan brown bear cub. All photos by Ron Garrison.

Map of the Zoo

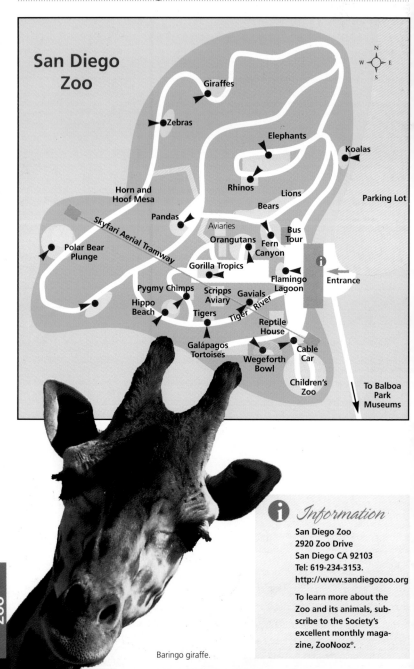

San Diego Zoo

N
W · E
S

Giraffes

Zebras

Elephants

Koalas

Rhinos

Lions

Horn and
Hoof Mesa

Bears

Parking Lot

Pandas

Aviaries

Bus
Tour

Skyfari Aerial Tramway

Orangutans

Fern
Canyon

Polar Bear
Plunge

Gorilla Tropics

Flamingo
Lagoon

Entrance

Pygmy Chimps

Scripps
Aviary

Gavials

Hippo
Beach

Tigers

Tiger River

Reptile
House

Galápagos
Tortoises

Wegeforth
Bowl

Cable
Car

Children's
Zoo

To Balboa
Park
Museums

Baringo giraffe.

ℹ *Information*

San Diego Zoo
2920 Zoo Drive
San Diego CA 92103
Tel: 619-234-3153.
http://www.sandiegozoo.org

To learn more about the
Zoo and its animals, sub-
scribe to the Society's
excellent monthly maga-
zine, ZooNooz®.

Zoo

The Skyfari Aerial Tramway ⏱ is best photographed as it rises over the duck pond, near the Children's Zoo.

Where

In Balboa Park, just north of the main buildings. Free parking off Park Blvd. From I-5, take the Pershing Drive exit north to Florida Drive and Zoo Place.

When ⏱

Morning is best as the animals are most active at this time. On hot summer afternoons, the animals may retreat to the shade and doze. Cooler weather and seasons (winter) are best. When it's raining the animals may seek shelter out of view.

You can easily spend an entire day here, if not more. To avoid the crowds, come early on weekdays. The pandas are very popular but not always on display—their exhibit times are posted at the entrance and there's a hotline at **1-888-MY PANDA**.

Pets are not permitted. Prices, exhibits and times subject to change.

Getting Around:

The best approach is to spend all day walking along the five miles of pathways. Make sure you bring comfortable walking shoes. There are exhibits and refreshments all over, so just aim for your favorite animals.

A good introduction is the 40-minute guided bus tour which departs from the Flamingo Lagoon area by the main entry plaza. The open-sided double-decker buses leave every few minutes on a three-mile round trip, and the commentary is fun and informative. There are good views of many animals, although you can't see

the pandas, pygmy chimpanzees, gorillas or sun bears.

Alternatively the Kangaroo Bus, which is also guided, follows the same route but allows you to ride all day and hop on and off at nine different stops.

The Skyfari® Aerial Tramway (extra charge) is a third-of-a mile trip to the far end of the Zoo. Starting from the main entrance, open-air gondolas whisk you over the treetops, 180 feet above the ground, to the Horn and Hoof Mesa. The ride is relaxing but doesn't give you close-up views of the animals.

Tip

Zoom in to the face. As with people, the most powerful shots of animals are usually just of the face. Use a 200mm or 300mm lens to zoom in.

Sumatran orangutan.

History of the Zoo

Derived from "It Began with a Roar!" by Dr. Harry M. Wegeforth and Neil Morgan.

"The account of the Zoo's founding is one of the most impressive stories of disinterested public service that San Diego or any other city may boast."
—San Diego Sun

"No one person gave so much of personal energy, interest, devotion and very life to the development of a public project as Doctor Harry gave to the creation of the Zoo."
—Tom Faulconer, Zoo Director.

"Practically alone, [Wegeforth] raised all the private funds with which the magnificent Zoo was built. He visualized and planned all of its unique features. He traveled at his own expense all over the world."
—From an early guidebook.

San Diego Zoo was founded by Dr. Harry M. Wegeforth (1882–1942), a local doctor who became a keen photographer.

The son of a German oil refiner, Wegeforth was born in Baltimore, MD. From an early age he became enthralled with animals, possibly from a visit to the Barnum and Bailey circus. In 1908, in search of a place to open a new medical practice, the newly-qualified doctor found his way to the warm climate of San Diego. He opened an office in downtown San Diego at Fifth and Broadway, and was later joined by his brother, Paul, in 1915.

In the book *It Began with a Roar!,* Wegeforth tells the story of the founding of the Zoo:

"On September 16, 1916, as I was returning to my office after performing an operation, I drove down Sixth Avenue and heard the roar of the lions in the cages at the Exposition then being held in Balboa Park. I turned to my brother, Paul, who was riding with me, and half jokingly, half wishfully, said, 'Wouldn't it be splendid if San Diego had a zoo! You know … I think I'll start one.'

"I had long nurtured the thought of a San Diego Zoo and now—suddenly—I decided to try to establish one. Dropping my brother at our office, I went down to the *San Diego Union* where I talked long and earnestly with Mr. Clarence McGrew, the city editor. Next morning, [an article proposing a zoo] appeared in the *Union*, prominently featured."

Three men offered support and October 2 the Zoological Society of San Diego (the "Society") was formed. Granted supervision of the Exposition animals, and given other animals by enthusiastic residents, the Society soon had a minor collection. The crew of a Navy ship even donated its pet bear—Caesar—which

Founder Dr. Harry Wegeforth riding one of the Zoo's first elephants in 1923.

The White Elephants

Wegeforth found it easier to pay for animals if he bought them on credit and then displayed them. In a famous incident, investor John D. Spreckels declined to pay for the Zoo's first elephants by joking that he only funded "white elephants." So Wegeforth had the beasts covered entirely in white powder. When Spreckels saw them, he laughed and promptly paid for the elephants and their compound.

"Watch out for this Wegeforth. If you're a patient, you get your tonsils or your appendix cut out. But if you're working on the Zoo, you get cut off at the pockets."
—John D. Spreckels.

"grew like a weed" and wrecked several cages. With a donation from Ellen Browning Scripps, a new type of restraint was built for Caesar—the Zoo's first open-moated enclosure.

More animals were acquired from the municipal zoo and a traveling circus. To transport them, Wegeforth drove with a bear in his car and rode elephants through the streets of San Diego.

In a battle to become automonous from the Park Commission, the Society gave its animals to the City in 1921 in exchange for permanent use of the present 126-acre location. The Zoo is thus owned by the people of San Diego and administered by the Zoological Society of San Diego.

Belle Benchley, who came to the San Diego Zoo in 1925 as a substitute bookkeeper, was promoted by Wegeforth to become the world's first woman zoo director. She wrote two bestsellers which promoted the Zoo and she campaigned persistently to make San Diego Zoo the first zoo outside of Australia to display koalas.

To counter the rise of animal dealers, Wegeforth established the Association of Zoological Parks and Aquariums to exchange animals and information.

Wegeforth traveled to every continent in search of animals and plants to build his zoo. He died in 1942, from pneumonia and malaria contracted while on an animal-buying expedition through India.

In 1972, the Society opened a second location near Escondido—the *San Diego Wild Animal Park*—where many of the larger animals could roam free.

Today the Society also maintains the Center for Reproduction of Endangered Species (CRES) which applies modern medical and scientific methods to save exotic animal species from extinction.

52

Tip
The flamingos ⊕ are the first animals you'll see. Their bright plumage makes for colorful photos. Concentrate on their most distinctive features—the long neck and slender legs.

Camera Den
Situated next to the clock tower at the main entrance, the Camera Den offers Kodak® film, batteries, single-use cameras, postcards, souvenirs and guidebooks.

Members of the Zoological Society of San Diego receive free admission for one year to the San Diego Zoo and San Diego Wild Animal Park. On Founder's Day (the first Monday in October—named in honor of founder Dr. Harry Wegeforth) the Zoo is free. The entire month of October is free for children age 11 and under.

Tip
Focus on the eyes. The most important part of any face is usually the eyes, so try to keep the eyes in focus. The mouth is the next-most important feature, and is easier to focus on with a manual focus camera.

No this isn't "Jurassic Park," it's an alligator. He's got his eye on you—don't stroke his teeth!

Zoo

Caribbean Flamingo ⊕

Greeting you at the entrance plaza is a display of flamingos. The Caribbean is the largest and most brightly hued of the six species of flamingo. The pink plumage is a result of the pigments present in their crustacean diet.

Tiger River ⊕

To the left of the flamingos is a small path into Tiger River. Recreating an Asian rainforest, this area was the Zoo's first bio-climactic exhibit. Bamboo and other plants are watered by mist-simulating monsoon rainfall. The winding path takes you past gharials, pythons, fishing cats and Malayan tapirs before reaching the eye-catching tigers.

Three windows allow you different views of Indo Chinese tigers. There are fewer than 2,000 Indo-Chinese tigers in the world.

Queensland Koala ⏱

Koalas are the unofficial symbol of San Diego. The Australian authorities were hesitant to allow the fragile marsupials outside of their native habitat. After much discussion, the San Diego Zoo was the first zoo outside of Australia to display koalas. Over 80 koalas have been born at the Zoo, making its collection of koalas the largest outside Australia.

Koalas are one of the most narrowly specialized mammals on Earth, eating only the leaves and young shoots of eucalyptus trees, and only those from 25 varieties of the more than 600 varieties native to Australia.

Nearby are Parma wallabies and Goodfellow's tree kangaroos.

Tip

Photograph the koalas first. Their exhibit has several purpose-built 'trees' for them to pose in, and a wooden deck for you to photograph from. The exhibit faces east so the best light is in the early morning. Use a 200mm lens to zoom in tight. A flash will help to light the koala's eyes and fur.
More koalas can be seen through viewing windows. Look out for Onya-Birri, a rare albino (white) koala.

Queensland koala.

Fern Canyon ⏱ is a verdant retreat. The best view is from the lower bridge looking up the canyon.

Left: North Chinese leopard. *Above:* Galápagos tortoise.

Galápagos Tortoise

These were Dr. Wegeforth's favorite animal. Nearby are American alligators and a komodo dragon.

Children's Zoo

The Zoo is dedicated to children and in this mini-zoo the conservationists of tomorrow can meet spider monkeys, tree kangaroos and naked mole-rats. There's a petting paddock and an area to watch chicks hatch.

Don't miss the nursery, used for hand-raising animals that have been injured or rejected by their mothers. If there are animals present, you can photograph the babies through glass windows.

Aviaries

There are three walk-through aviaries, which allow you to watch and photograph exotic birds. The multi-level Scripps Aviary is the oldest and largest. Carefully placed feeders allow some very close-up viewing.

Picture credits in this section:

© 1999 Zoological Society of San Diego: Ron Gordon Garrison: 44 (also back cover), 46, 47, 48, 49 (bus), 52 (flamingos), 53 (koalas), 54, 55, 56 (gorillas), 58 (upper), 61; Ken Kelley: 44, 52 (tiger). 51. For photo fees and order forms, write to the San Diego Zoo Photo Lab, Box 551, San Diego CA 92112, or call 619-231-1515, ext. 4401.

© 1999 PhotoSecrets Publishing: Andrew Hudson: 49 (Skyfari and orangutan), 52 (alligator), 53 (Fern Canyon), 56 (chimp and show), 57, 58 (center and lower), 59, 60.

Tip

Be careful of shadows. **Many animals are dark-skinned and the slightest shadow will appear black on film, with no detail. Try to get an even spread of sunlight on the face.**

Gorilla Tropics®

The recently remodeled Gorilla Tropics (above) displays magnificent lowland gorillas at a simulated African rainforest.

Pygmy Chimps at Bonobo Road

This is the first exhibition in the U.S. of these endangered pygmy chimps. In their native Republic of Congo they are called 'bonobos.' Bonobos live in female-dominated groups. There are fewer than 100 in captivity.

Shows

Live animal shows are presented at the Wegeforth Bowl and the Hunte Amphitheater.

Tip
Use a neutral background.
Try to photograph the animals with a simple, mid-toned background. With giraffes, use the mid-toned tree leaves rather than sky as a background. A bright sky may confuse your light meter and make the shot underexposed. A complicated background will distract from your subject.

Horn and Hoof Mesa

On the flat plains of the west side roam several hoofed species from Africa such as zebras and giraffes.

Tip
Capture expression. To add life and interest to your photographs, wait for the animals to interact with each other and express character and emotion.

Borneo orangutan

Hippo Beach℠ 1995

With a 105-foot-long observation window, this exhibit allows you to photograph two hippos, Funani and Jabba, underwater. The two-ton creatures seem awkward on land but are graceful and lithe when swimming in their 150,000 gallon pool. Now you can appreciate why Walt Disney cast hippos as ballerinas!

Nearby are three more hippos, this time made of sand and glue. Lifeguard Mitch, Kahuna Kevin and Surfer Sally are sand sculptures by Gerry Kirk, 1996.

Polar Bear Plunge℠ 1996

Come face-to-face with earth's largest carnivore! Designed as a 2.2-acre summer tundra habitat, this is one of the largest polar bear exhibits in the world. A two-level underwater viewing area allows you to watch the playful bears swimming and jumping in their 12-foot-deep, 130,000-gallon pool of chilled water. You can photograph the animals through the 'bear-proof' acrylic window.

Also displayed in the complex are Siberian reindeer, arctic foxes and a variety of arctic birds.

Tip

Include people for scale and reaction. Stand a few feet back from the glass to include some people in the shot. Try to capture that eye-to-eye contact between the hippo or polar bear and a person. Children usually make the best subjects. A fill-flash will illuminate the otherwise darkened people. Shoot at an angle to the glass to reduce reflection from the flash.

Photographing the Zoo

By Ron Gordon Garrison

Ron Gordon Garrison is the Photo Services Manager for the Zoological Society of San Diego. He has been photographing the animals of San Diego Zoo and San Diego Wild Animal Park since 1965 and supplies most of the images for the Society's magazine, ZooNooz®.

If you wish to sell or commercially reproduce images you have taken of the Zoo animals, you need permission first. Send a written request to:

The Zoological Society
 of San Diego
Public Relations Department
P.O. Box 551
San Diego CA 92112-0551
Tel: 619-685-3291
Fax: 619-557-3970

You are free to use a tripod and flash in the zoo, unless advised otherwise. Some animals, particularly gorillas, are sensitive to flash so there may be 'no flash' signs. As always, be careful with a tripod as people may trip over the legs.

Zoo

I've been photographing the zoo now for over 30 years, and still I love every minute. There's always something new to capture—a new animal or attraction —and the scenery is fabulous. I've traveled to many countries in Africa and Asia to photograph for the Society, but I've never found a better place to photograph so much wildlife than right here in San Diego.

I recommend using an SLR camera with a variety of lenses, depending upon the view. Simplifying the view is very important. The most powerful images are made when you crop tightly into the face of one animal. For this I use a 135–300mm lens, set at the widest aperture, and sometimes with a 2x convertor. With a long lens, a tripod is necessary to get sharp images. Autofocus is very useful as the animals move quite a lot.

Using a flash can highlight the face and add a twinkle to the eyes. However, if you have a built-in flash, it's usually better to switch it off as it creates glare on glass and doesn't work on subjects farther than about ten feet away from you.

Light meters are 'fooled' by very bright or very dark subjects. When photographing a white polar bear on a white background, automatic exposure will make the image turn out gray. To retain the white, overexpose by a stop (+1 exposure compensation). Similarly, if you're photographing the face of a black gorilla, underexpose by a stop (-1).

How to shoot through glass or wire

Several of our animals are exhibited behind glass, which can produce glare. To avoid this, shoot at an angle to the glass. Alternatively, shoot straight on and get very close to the surface. Don't touch the glass as you can can scratch it, instead use your hands or a rubber lens hood as a buffer. If you're using a flash, use a PC cord and hold it off to one side of the camera.

To shoot through wire, get close to the wire and use your widest aperture.

Right: Scarlet macaw.

Ten Tips

"The [35mm] camera is for life and for people, the swift and intense moments of life."
—*Ansel Adams.*

Include people

Magazine picture editors always like people in the shot. It gives the viewer a human connection, a sense of being there, and a sense of scale.

Photographs evoke emotion and empathy comes with someone's face. Avoid crowds and simplify the shot down to one person. The young and old are preferred subjects, with, respectively, their innocent expressions and weather-worn faces. People make your shots warm, friendly and person-able. Just like you are.

Have you ever got your photos back only to discover that something that looked awe-inspiring at the time looks dull on paper? This is because your eye needs some reference point to judge scale. Add a person, car or something of known size to indicate the magnitude of the scenery.

1. Hold It Steady

A problem with many photographs is that they're blurry. Avoid 'camera shake' by holding the camera steady. Use both hands, resting your elbows on your chest, or use a wall for support. Relax: don't tense up. You're a marksman/woman holding a gun and it must be steady to shoot.

2. Put The Sun Behind You

A photograph is all about light so always think of how the light is striking your subject. The best bet is to move around so that the sun is behind you and to one side. This front-lighting brings out color and shades, and the slight angle (side-lighting) produces some shadow to indicate texture and form.

3. Get Closer

The best shots are simple so move closer and remove any clutter from the picture. If you look at most 'people' shots they don't show the whole body so you don't need to either. Move close, fill the frame with just the face, or even overflow it. Give your shot some impact. Use a zoom to crop the image tighter.

4. Choose A Format

Which way you hold the camera affects what is emphasized in your shot. Use a vertical format to emphasize height, for a tall tree or building. Use a horizontal format to show the dramatic sweep of some mountains.

5. Include People

Photographs solely of landscape and buildings are enjoyable to take but often dull to look at. Include some of your friends, companions, family or even people passing by to add human interest. If there's no one around, include yourself with the self-timer.

Depth

Always include some pointer about depth. A photograph is two-dimensional but we want it to appear three-dimensional. If you're shooting a background (mountains) include a strong foreground (people).

Use a wide-angle lens for exaggerated depth. With a 20mm to 28mm lens, get just a few feet from your subject and, with a small aperture (large f-number), include an in-focus deep background too. This exaggerated 'hyperfocal' perspective is used in a lot of magazine shots. What impact!

Alternatively you can remove all depth by using a long, telephoto lens. This compresses or compacts the image, making your 3-D subject appear flat.

Always centering your subject can get dull. Use the 'rule of thirds' to add variety and interest.

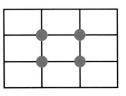

● = suggested placement of subject in frame.

6. Consider Variety

You may take the greatest shots but if they're all the same type or style, they may be dull to look at. Spice up your collection by adding variety. Include landscapes and people shots, close ups and wide angles, good weather and bad weather. Take personal shots that remember the 'being there'—friends that you meet, your hotel/campsite, transportation, street or hiking signposts.

7. Add Depth

Depth is an important quality of good photographs. We want the viewer to think that they're not looking at a flat picture, but through a window, into a three-dimensional world. Add pointers to assist the eye. If your subject is a distant mountain, add a person or a tree in the foreground. A wide angle lens can exaggerate this perspective.

8. Use Proportion

The beauty of an image is often in it's proportions. A popular technique with artists is called the 'rule of thirds' or the 'golden mean.' Imagine the frame divided into thirds, both horizontally and vertically, like a Tic-Tac-Toe board. Now place your subject on one of the lines or intersections.

9. Search For Details

It's always tempting to use a wide angle lens and 'get everything in.' However this can be too much and you may loose the impact. Instead zoom in with a longer lens and find some representative detail. A shot of an entire Sequoia tree just looks like a tree. But a shot of just the wide base, with a person for scale, is more powerful.

10. Position The Horizon

Where you place the horizon in your shot affects what is emphasized. To show the land, use a high horizon. To show the sky, use a low horizon. Be creative.

Advanced Tips

"Emphasis on technique is justified only so far as it will simplify and clarify the statement of the photographer's concept."
—*Ansel Adams*

Simple Clean Layout

A good shot focuses your attention on the subject by using a sparse background and a simple but interesting composition. Always remove clutter from the picture—this is a real skill. Like a musician, it's always difficult to make things look easy. Zoom in, get close, get to eye level, find a simple backdrop, look for balance.

Bold Solid Colors

'Stock-quality' images make great use of color. Look for solid primary colors: bright 'sports-car' red, emerald green, lightning yellow, and ocean blue. Use a polarizer to bring out the colors. Avoid patterns—keep it simple. Bright afternoon sunlight will add warmth.
Alternatively, look for 'color harmony'—scenes restricted to similar tones and colors, or even a single color. This presents a calm, restful image where the eye plays with the differing shades and intensities. Look for pastels, cream, or delicate shades.

1. Use a Narrow Tonal Range

Photographic film can't handle a wide tonal range. When you photograph very bright things and very dark things together—sunlight in water and shadows in trees—the film will lose all the detail and you'll end up with stark, overexposed white and total underexposed black. Instead, look for mid-tones with little difference between the brightest and darkest highlights. Flowers, trees and people are often best photographed on overcast days as the dispersed light fills in shadows.

Your eye can handle a difference in brightness (a 'dynamic range') of about 2,000:1 (11 camera 'stops'). Print film is limited to no more than 64:1 (5 stops) and slide film is even worse, at 8:1 (3 stops). Ansel Adams' 'Zone System' divided light levels into 11 'zones' and advised using a narrow zone (or tonal) range.

2. Work The Subject, Baby!

As film directors say, film is cheap (although it's not always their money!). Work the subject and take different shots from different angles. The more you take, the more likely you are to get a good one. Don't be afraid to take five shots and throw four away. Find different, unusual viewpoints. Shoot from high and from low. It's often said that the only difference between a professional photographer and an amateur photographer is that the professional throws more shots away. I use about 4 shots from each roll of 36. *National Geographic* magazine uses only 1 out of every 1,000 shots taken.

3. Hyperfocal

A popular 'pro' technique is to capture great depth by combining a close foreground and deep background. Use a wide angle lens (20-28mm), get a few inches from the foreground (often flowers), put the horizon high in the frame. Using a small aperture (f22) keeps everything in focus ('hyperfocal'). Use a hyperfocal chart to correspond distance with aperture, or just use the smallest aperture (highest f-number) possible.

Dramatic Lighting

Photographs that win competitions are often ones that make interesting use of light. Look out for beams of light shining through clouds, trees or windows, long shadows, and the effect of side- and backlighting. Shoot in the warm golden 'magic hours' of early morning and late afternoon.

Preparation

A great shot takes time. Scout out the area, make mental notes of important features, unusual and interesting angles, and changing crowd levels. Take time to prepare the shot. Get there before the best time of day, clean your lenses, set up a tripod or mini-tripod, add a cable release, try out different filters, wait for a good foreground, and talk with people who may be in the shot so that they're comfortable and will pose well.

"Chance favors the prepared mind."
—Louis Pasteur.

4. Expose For Highlights

When a scene has a mixture of very bright and very dark areas, the light meter in your camera will have difficulty finding the right exposure. In such high-contrast shots, try to expose for the highlights. To do this, walk up to, zoom in to, or spot meter on the most important bright area (a face, the sky, some architectural detail) and half-depress the shutter release button to hold the exposure (exposure lock). Then recompose and take the shot. To be on the safe side, take several 'bracketed' shots (see below).

5. Under- (over-) Expose for Deeper Colors
SLR only

On slide film, a slightly underexposed image (on print film, a slightly overexposed image) can give deeper, more saturated colors. The deeper color also makes the subject appear heavier. To underexpose on a manual SLR camera, select the next shutter speed up (for example 1/250 when 1/125 is recommended by the meter). On an automatic camera, set the exposure compensation dial to -1/2 or -1. Similarly, you can underexpose for paler, lighter images.

The effect is dependent upon your camera and film so try some test runs to find the best combination. On my camera—a Minolta X-700 with Fuji Velvia film—the recommended exposure works best and underexposure just loses detail.

6. Bracketing   *SLR only*

When in doubt about the correct exposure, take several 'bracketed' shots. You 'bracket' around a shot by taking one regular shot, then a second shot slightly darker (-1 stop) and a third shot slightly lighter (+1 stop). Slide film is more sensitive than print film and you can detect exposure differences down to a third of a stop. Professionals therefore often bracket at +/- 1/2 stop. Some cameras offer bracketing as an automatic feature.

Camera Stores

San Diego has two main centers for camera equipment—Nelson's and George's. Both carry a wide array of cameras, accessories, rental equipment and film. Nelson's is the most accessible for tourists, being just north of downtown San Diego on India Street at Fir Street, in Little Italy. George's lies northeast of Balboa Park, on 30th Street at University Avenue, in North Park.

Camera Stores

Nelson Photo Supplies   619-234-6621
1909 India, Little Italy

George's Camera   619-297-3544
3837 30th Street, North Park

Camera Mart   619-283-7321
3311 Adams Ave, North Park

Point Loma Camera   619-224-2719
1310 Rosecrans, nr Shelter Island

Bob Davis' Camera   619-459-7355
7720 Fay Ave, La Jolla

La Mesa Camera   619-466-0567
8285 La Mesa Blvd., La Mesa

Chula Vista Photo   619-425-2400
367 3rd Avenue, Chula Vista

Carlsbad Village Camera 760-720-0108
457 Carlsbad Vilage. Dr., Carlsbad

Oceanside Photo   760-722-3348
1024 Mission Avenue, Oceanside

North County Camera   760-737-6002
945 W. Valley Pkwy, Escondido

Camera Repair

Kurt's Camera Repair   619-286-1810
7811 Mission Gorge Road

Professional Photo   619-277-3700
7910 Raytheon Rd, Kearny Mesa

Nolan's Camera Clinic   619-581-3777
4454 Ingraham, Pacific Beach

North County Repair   760-722-5936
1024 Mission Avenue, Oceanside

Professional Developing (E6)

Chrome (2 stores)   619-233-3456
2345 Kettner, Little Italy
6150 Lusk Blvd., Sorrento Valley

Chromacolor   619-232-9900
1953 India Street, Little Italy

Masters Developing   619-558-4546
9833 Pacific Height Blvd.

Film Express   619-574-1875
1268 University Ave., Hillcrest

Point Loma Camera   619-224-2719
1310 Rosecrans, nr Shelter Island

Color Craft   619-234-4668
636 7th Ave., downtown

Photo Express   619-296-3385
3572 Hancock Street, Point Loma

Pacific Coast Photo   619-454-9137
5661 La Jolla Blvd, Birdrock

Professional Enlargements

Award Photo Imaging   619-549-3900
7686 Miramar Road, Mira Mesa

Digital n Beyond   619-565-0556
4820 Mercury Street

Giant Photo Service   619-232-1371
544 7th Avenue

Mesa Photo X   619-271-1950
9530 Padgett Street

Photodyne   619-292-0140
7012 Convoy Court

Camera Clubs

Escondido Camera Club 760-749-1421
Joslyn Senior Center, Escondido

Fallbrook Camera Club 760-731-6236
Silvergate Retirement Residence

Rancho Bernado C.C. 760-744-8898
3rd floor, Pomerado Hospital

Sierra Club Photo Div. 619-466-3371
Tierrasanta Rec. Center

Underwater Photo Soc. 619-566-6170
Scripps Instit'n of Oceanography

Vista Camera Club 760-757-2411
Green Valley Mobile Home Park

The following clubs meet in Balboa
Park in the Photographic Arts Building,
by the Spanish Village Art Center:

Darkroomers	619-224-7616
Foto Learners	619-286-8436
Photo Arts	619-582-3667
Poly Photo	619-279-9726
Stereo (3D)	619-262-2940
Showette	619-444-1262
Daytime	619-582-3667
Lens Art	619-270-2882
Photo Naturalists	619-239-7967
Movie Makers	619-444-1262
Showmasters	619-279-9726
Tuesday Workshop	619-464-1744

Associations

Southern California Association of
Camera Clubs (SCACC). Represents 19
clubs listed above. 619-232-1321.

The Professional Photographers of San
Diego County meet at the Four Points
Sheraton. 619-743-4130.

Publications

"California Photographer" newsletter.
Tel: 760-324-7499   www.calphoto.com

Museums

MoPA   619-238-7559
Museum of Photographic Arts
1649 El Prado, Balboa Park

Other Information

San Diego Visitor Information Center
11 Horton Plaza (1st Ave & F Street),
San Diego, CA 92101.
Tel: 619-236-1212.
Hours: Mon–Sat., 8:30am–5pm;
(Sun 11–5, Jun–Aug)

Mission Bay Visitor Information
2688 E Mission Bay Drive,
San Diego, CA 92109.
619-276-8200. Hours:9am–sunset.

Information Centers
San Diego Convention and

Visitors Bureau	619-236-1212
Gaslamp Quarter	619-233-5227
Balboa Park	619-239-0512
Coronado	619-228-7049
Carlsbad	760-931-8400
Chula Vista	619-425-4444
Oceanside	800-350-7873
North County	800-848-3336
Tijuana	619-428-1422
Travelers Aid Society	619-232-7991
Bus and Trolley	619-234-1060
Spotlight SD (events)	619-551-6464
California Concierge	619-294-7744
Discovering San Diego	619-578-7588
International Info. Ctr.	619-232-8583
Weather	619-289-1212

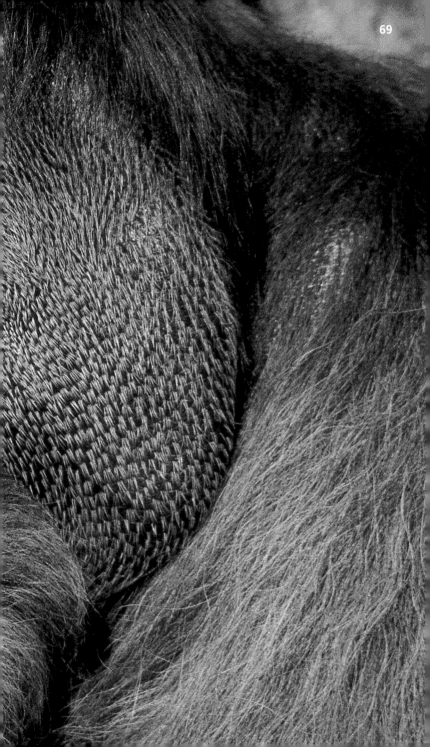

Order Form

Other PhotoSecrets books:

- ❑ PhotoSecrets Balboa Park $10.95
  First edition, 72 pages
- ❑ PhotoSecrets San Diego $18.95
  First edition, 336 pages
- ❑ PhotoSecrets Yosemite $ 7.95
  First edition, 72 pages
- ❑ PhotoSecrets San Francisco $16.95
  and Northern California
  First edition, 352 pages

Send comments to:
feedback@photosecrets.com
PhotoSecrets Publishing
Box 13554,
La Jolla CA 92039-3554 USA

Visit the website at:
photosecrets.com

Quantity discounts available. Prices may change with future editions. For orders shipped to San Diego County, add 7.75% sales tax; for orders shipped elsewhere in California add 7.25%. Add $4 shipping ($6.95 for overseas orders) for the first book, plus $1 for each additional book. Make your check payable to "PhotoSecrets Publishing" and send to:

PhotoSecrets
P.O. Box 13554
La Jolla CA 92039-3554

Distributed to the trade by National Book Network (NBN). For more information call 800-622-8284.

Travel Guides for Travel Photography

Index

A

Aerospace Museum .38
Alcazar Garden 22

B

Balboa Park Club . .40
Balboa, Vasco N. de 13
Botanical Building . .30

C

Cabrillo Bridge 16
California Building .18
California Tower . . .18
Camera Clubs 67
Camera Stores 66
Carousel 34
Casa de Balboa 27
Casa del Prado 34
Churrigueresque . . .25

E

El Cid statue 24
El Prado 22
Evenson, Bea 15

F

Fountains
    Bea Evenson 32
    Plaza de Panama .24

G

Goodhue, Bertram .13

H

History
    Balboa Park 12
    San Diego Zoo . .50
House of Charm . . .26
House of Hospitality 26

L

Lawn Bowling 16
Lily Pond 31
Lindbergh, Charles .39

M

Maps
    Balboa Park 4
    San Diego Zoo . .48
Marston House 42
Museums:
    Aerospace 38
    Art 25
    Automotive 41
    Champions 41
    Free days 43
    Man 18
    Marston House . .42
    Model Railroad . .27
    Natural History . .38
    Photographic Arts 27
    San Diego History 27
    Space Theater . .32
    Timken 27

O

Old Globe Theater .22
Organ Pavilion 37

P

Palisades Building . .40
Palm Canyon 37
Pan America Plaza . .40
Pandas, Giant 44
Photography tips . . .62
Plateresque 25
Plaza de Panama . . .24
Plaza de Balboa 32

R

Railroad museum . .27
Reuben H. Fleet Space
    Theater 32
Rose Garden 35

S

San Diego Aerospace
    Museum 38
San Diego Automotive
    Museum 41
San Diego Museum
    of Art 25
San Diego Museum
    of Man 18
San Diego Natural
    History Museum .33
San Diego Zoo 44
    Gorilla Tropics . . .56
    Hippo Beach 58
    Polar Bear Plunge 58
    Tiger River 52
Sessions, Kate O. . . .13
Simon Edison
    Centre 22
Space Theater 32
Spirit of St. Louis . .39
Spreckels Organ 37

T

Tips 62, 64
Tours 43

W

Wegeforth, Dr. H . .50

Z

Zoo 44

Also available:

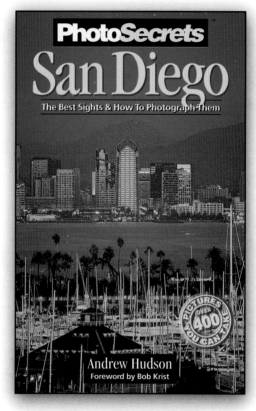

ISBN 0-9653087-3-1 • 336 pages
Available from bookstores and giftshops.

Visit the website:
photosecrets.com

Travel Guides for Travel Photography

3504